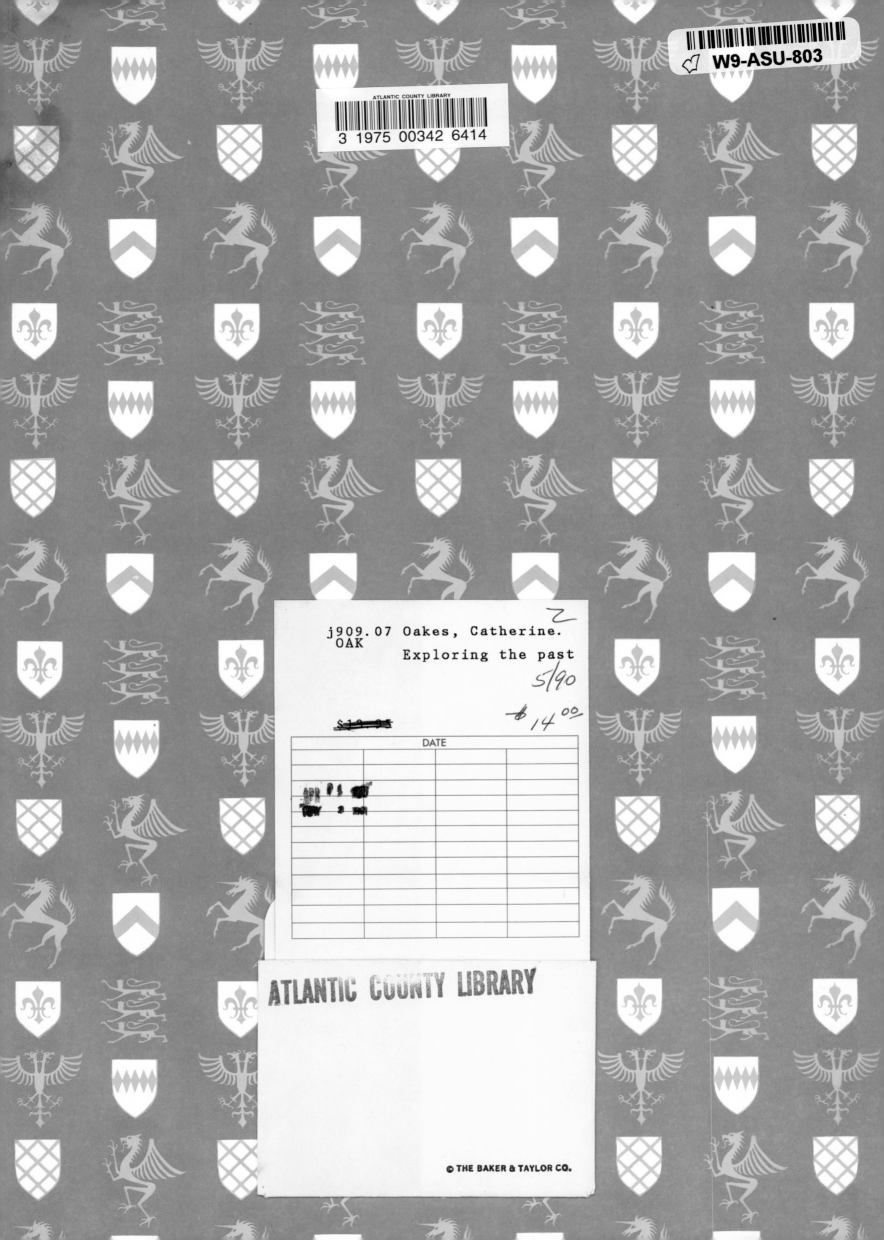

First published 1989 by The Hamlyn Publishing Group Limited
Copyright © 1989 by The Hamlyn Publishing Group Limited

Library of Congress Cataloging-in-Publication Data
Oakes, Catherine.
Exploring the past : the Middle Ages / by Catherine Oakes :
illustrated by Stephen Biesty.
p.   cm.
"Gulliver books."
Includes index.
Summary: An overview of life in the Middle Ages,
describing the arts and learning, religion, trading
and exploration, nobility, and life in the country,
in the towns, and in the wider world.
ISBN 0-15-200451-3
1. Civilization, Medieval — Juvenile literature.
[1. Civilization, Medieval. 2. Middle Ages.] I. Biesty, Stephen,
ill. II. Title.
CB351.023 1989
909.07 — dc19   88-30075

Produced by Mandarin Offset
Printed and bound in Hong Kong

First U.S. edition 1989
A B C D E